TABLE OF CONTENTS

WHAT'S THAT GLOW?

SHINE TIME!

Does all this glowing light get hot, like a light bulb? Nope! The glow made by animals is called *cold light*.

KNOW THE GLOW!

Pay attention! Most animals only use their light for short bursts. Fireflies are the most famous glowing animals. They flicker and flash several times per second.

Animals of all kinds light up the worlds they live in. Put on your shades and get ready for a light-filled look at animals!

- The word of the day is **bioluminescence**. That means light from a living thing. Most glowing animals use bioluminescence to make light.

- How does it work? Chemistry does the job! Stuff called *luciferin* in the animals' bodies mixes with oxygen. A **chemical reaction** makes the luciferin glow so you can see it!

- Another way animals glow is with **fluorescence**. That means the animals don't create the glow. Instead, their skin or fur reacts to **ultraviolet (UV) light**.

WHY DO THEY GLOW?

It's not just for show! All across the animal kingdom, animals use their glowing light powers to stay alive!

They're saying hello! Some jellyfish light up to communicate with each other.

SHINE TIME!

Sharks that glow are probably trying to hide. Scientists think the lantern shark's glowing skin makes the fish hard to see against the sunlight from above.

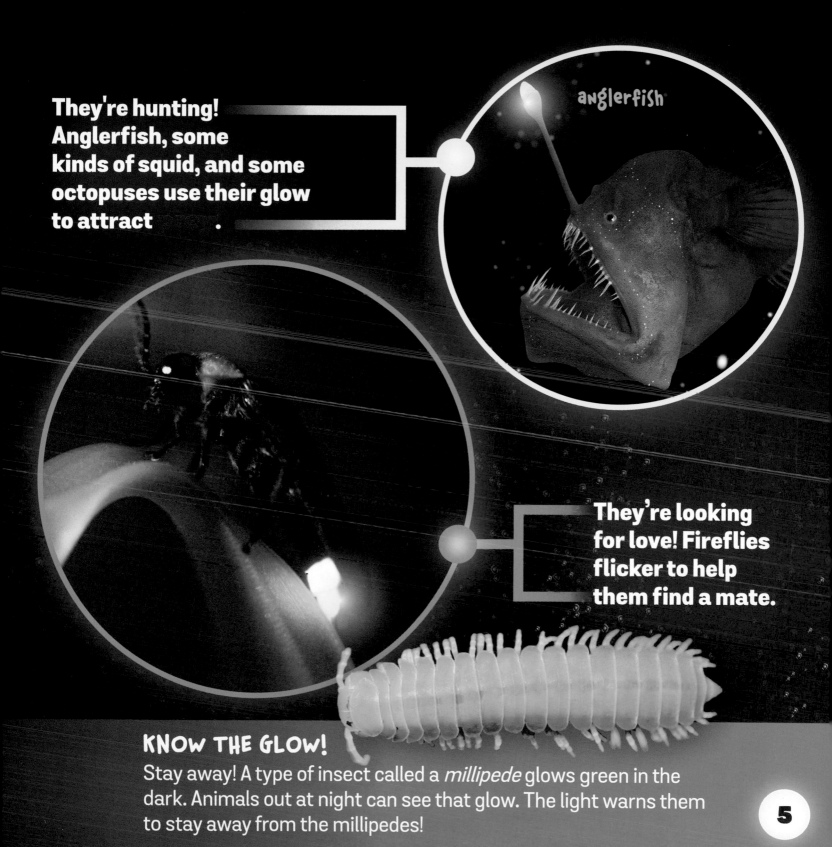

They're hunting! Anglerfish, some kinds of squid, and some octopuses use their glow to attract   .

anglerfish

They're looking for love! Fireflies flicker to help them find a mate.

KNOW THE GLOW!

Stay away! A type of insect called a *millipede* glows green in the dark. Animals out at night can see that glow. The light warns them to stay away from the millipedes!

FIREFLY

KNOW THE GLOW!

Adult fireflies don't get all the fun. Some species of this insect have eggs that glow! Even some of the **larvae** (baby fireflies) can be an eerie green too!

These famous flickering insects shine brightly in our collection of glowing animals!

● Fireflies blink fastest when they are looking for a mate. Both males and females flash to meet each other in the dark.

● Yellow, orange, or even green! Different firefly species put out different colored light.

● Fireflies are not flies . . . they are beetles! More than 2,000 types of fireflies flit around the world.

SHINE TIME!

Bonus! The chemical that gives fireflies light also makes them taste nasty! This helps protect the fireflies from **predators**.

ANGLERFISH

SHINE TIME!

Female anglerfish rule!
Only the females of
this species have the
glowing lure.

Fishing in the dark? That's not a problem for this deep-sea hunter.

- Anglerfish live more than 1,000 ft. (304.8 m) below the surface of the sea. It is so deep that there is no sunlight.

- It has a body part with a glowing end. Smaller fish come to the light. When they get close ... snap! Lunchtime!

- More than 200 species of anglerfish have been found. Most are less than 1 ft. (.3 m) long, but some can be more than 3 ft. (.9 m)!

KNOW THE GLOW!

This is an example of organisms helping organisms. Anglerfish don't glow on their own. Instead, glowing **bacteria** live on the end of the fish's dangling lure!

JELLYFISH

SHINE TIME!

Glow or no glow, jellyfish are among the oldest animals in the world. Some species have been around for more than 700 million years!

KNOW THE GLOW!

One scientist guessed that nine out of ten types of animals that live in the very deep, dark ocean can glow in some way.

Ooey, gooey, squishy, squashy . . . but also elegant, beautiful, and colorful: Let's meet the surprising jellyfish!

- Jellyfish are invertebrates; that means animals without backbones. They are also not fish—they are called *zooplankton*.

- Their bodies are 98 percent water along with some nerves and a digestive system.

- Jellyfish that glow usually do it to scare predators or attract prey of their own.

MORE JELLYFISH

SHINE TIME!

Scientists around the world use a glowing chemical made from jellyfish. It lets them study how other things glow by making those other things light up!

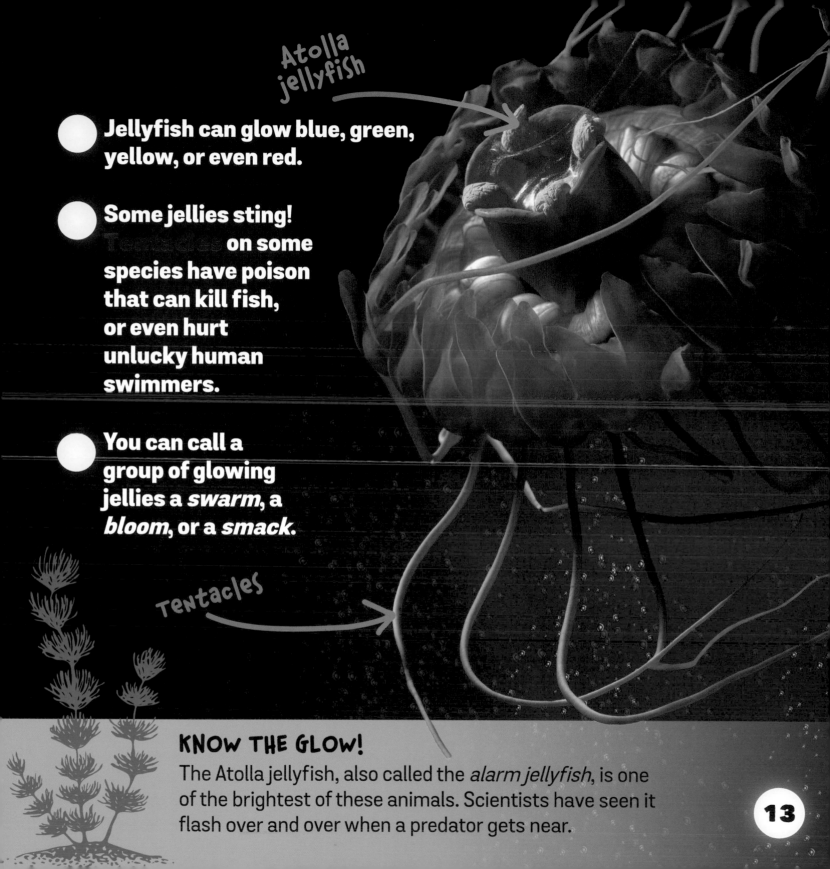

Atolla jellyfish

- Jellyfish can glow blue, green, yellow, or even red.

- Some jellies sting! Tentacles on some species have poison that can kill fish, or even hurt unlucky human swimmers.

- You can call a group of glowing jellies a *swarm*, a *bloom*, or a *smack*.

Tentacles

KNOW THE GLOW!

The Atolla jellyfish, also called the *alarm jellyfish*, is one of the brightest of these animals. Scientists have seen it flash over and over when a predator gets near.

LANTERN SHARK

SHINE TIME!

At only about 4 in. (10.2 cm) long, the dwarf lantern shark is the smallest shark species!

As if sharks were not cool enough, scientists now know that some glow in the dark!

- The lantern shark was named for a type of lamp used by people!

- Some might use their light to "talk" to each other. The patterns of the light cells might be sending messages to other lantern sharks.

- The velvet belly lantern shark can make sharp spines on its back light up. One scientist called them *light sabers*!

KNOW THE GLOW!

Camouflage! Some lantern sharks glow to hide themselves amid the light flashing down from the sea's surface. You can't eat what you can't see!

KITEFIN SHARK

Comparison between non-glowing and glowing shark.

KNOW THE GLOW!
Studying glow-in-the-dark animals is hard to do in a lab. During a 2020 trip to find out more about kitefins, explorers put them in tanks on ships at sea, right after they caught the fish, to study the glow up-close for the first time.

It's big, has sharp teeth, and glows! But don't worry, this shark doesn't bother people (but it sure is cool to look at)!

- Kitefin sharks are the largest vertebrates (animals with a spine) that glow.

- They live in oceans where the water is 660–3,300 ft. (201–1,006 m) deep.

- The kitefin shark glows blue . . . but don't confuse it with another species of fierce fish called a *blue shark* (which doesn't glow)!

dorsal

SHINE TIME!

Most sharks that glow, light up on their bottoms or sides. Scientists were surprised to find that kitefin shark's *dorsal* fins also glow!

FIREFLY SQUID

SHINE TIME!

Glow lovers get rides out to the glowing sea. They can also visit the world's only squid museum in Namerikawa, Japan.

Tourists can visit Japan to see these tiny glowing squid!

- From March to June, these neon-blue squid rise up from the deep waters to find mates at night.

- Together, tens of thousands of the glowing squid turn the water electric blue.

- In Japanese, the name for these tasty light-up squid is *hotaru-ika*.

KNOW THE GLOW!

Bright, glowing blue squid are pretty easy to catch. During the squid's annual light time, fishermen haul them in using giant nets. Some people eat these little gooey animals raw!

KNOW THE GLOW!

Lanternfish are everywhere! One scientist thinks that if you added them all up, lanternfish would make up more than half of the weight of all deep-sea fish in the world!

There are so many glowing lanternfish in the deep, dark sea that they are like millions of fishy light bulbs!

- They glow, usually green, to attract the tiny prey that they eat.

- Lanternfish also use their light to signal to mates.

- There are more than 200 types of lanternfish, ranging from 1 to 12 in. (2.5 to 30.4 cm) long.

SHINE TIME!

During the day, many types of lanternfish rise to the surface. They light up as they go. When looking up from below, predators have a hard time seeing the glowing fish against the sea lit by sunlight!

BRITTLE STAR

SHINE TIME!

Each arm has tiny tubelike "feet." Together, these feet help move the brittle star across rock and the seafloor in search of food.

These deep-sea creatures can not only glow . . . they can grow (new arms)!

- A brittle star has five arms coming from its body at the center. Species can be a few inches across to more than 1 ft. (.3 m)!

- If attacked, some species flash a bright green. Warning! Do not eat!

- They can leave behind a glowing arm while they escape. Don't worry— these animals can grow new arms!

KNOW THE GLOW!

Brittle stars are related to sea stars, sea cucumbers, and sea urchins. They are all types of animals without backbones called *echinoderms* .

GLOWING SEA SLUG

KNOW THE GLOW!
Believe it or not, these **nudibranchs** poop out of an organ
on the side of their bodies . . . not the bottom!

What is shaped like a fish, swims like a fish, has fins like a fish . . . but isn't a fish? It's a slug!

- This is a type of sea slug or nudibranch called a *phylliroe* . . . and it glows blue when bothered or startled!

- Most nudibranchs are squishy and ooze along like land slugs. Phylliroe evolved to be shaped and move like a fish.

- These glowing slugs, which are about 2 in. (5 cm) long, live in the deep ocean and eat jellies.

SHINE TIME!

When these animals are young, they attach themselves to larger jellies . . . and eat them!

PYROSOME

Pyrosome with a feeding shrimp

SHINE TIME!

Some scientists think the tiny zooids, which can light up one by one, use their glow to "talk" with other zooids. If one giant pyrosome lights up, others nearby will too!

When the water warms up, glowing purple tubes come out. Why? No one knows!

- **Pyrosomes are actually colonies of thousands of tiny animals called *zooids*. They join together to form tubes that can be from 1 to 30 ft. (.3 to 9.1 m) long.**

- **They look like bumpy, hairy, slightly purple cucumbers or purple fuzzy socks.**

- **Pyrosomes are very rarely seen until an area of the ocean warms up. Then they can arrive by the millions!**

zooids

KNOW THE GLOW!
The zooids that combine to form these tubes are not much bigger than the point of a pencil! They each eat by sucking in water and spewing it back out. All that spewing moves the giant pyrosome around.

SIPHONOPHORE

KNOW THE GLOW!

In 2005, a scientist discovered a type of siphonophore that dangles glowing red tentacles like fishing lures.

This animal has a name that sounds like a sea monster, but it's not!

- Siphonophores are long, thin, gooey, and boneless. Many are more than 40 ft. (12.2 m) long.

- They are actually colonies, or gatherings, of hundreds or thousands of smaller animals, each with a job to do to help the others.

- Siphonophores use their blue–green glow to scare predators and can also break up into many parts to escape trouble. Most of the broken parts can then live on their own.

SHINE TIME!

Some species can look like a string of holiday lights floating in the water.

DRAGONFISH

SHINE TIME!

When the inky-black dragonfish opens its mouth to snap up prey, it hides. Its teeth are see-through!

In the deep, dark ocean, one predator has a secret weapon . . . it's invisible to nearly all of its prey!

- Dragonfish are about 8–12 in. (20.3–30.5 cm) long and can live more than 6,000 ft. (1,828.8 m) deep in the ocean.

- Unlike most deep–sea fish, a dragonfish can see the color red. Its body actually glows that color.

- Using the light from its red body, dragonfish can swim right up to prey . . . which can't see the predator's red–lit body!

photophore

KNOW THE GLOW!

Like sharks, dragonfish use **photophores** to create their light. Dragonfish photophores are located under each eye to work as searchlights.

GLOWWORM

KNOW THE GLOW!
The glowworm caves are popular for tourists to visit. Visitors walk in to see a glowing blue display of hundreds of strands of gnat goo!

To see this amazing glowing animal display, you've got to make a *loooong* trip!

- Glowworms live only in a few caves in New Zealand and Australia. The biggest caves are called Te *Anau* and *Waitomo*.

- They're not worms. They are a type of fungus gnat, which is an insect. The babies, or larvae, of this gnat cling to cave ceilings.

- Glowworms are like spiders too! The larvae lower glowing strands of sticky goo from the top of their cave. Tiny insects get stuck in the goo and become glowworm food.

SHINE TIME!

After about nine months, the larvae change into adult gnats. Adults don't glow though!

close-up of glowing goo

GLOWING CLICK BEETLE

SHINE TIME!

When these insects are flipped onto their back, they use muscles to go back onto their feet. As they flip, they make a loud clicking sound.

These are the only insects with headlights! Add in their famous click, and it's a sound-and-light show!

- Glowing click beetles, about 1 in. (2.5 cm) long, live in the southern United States and northern Mexico.

- Two small body parts near its head can glow bright green.

- The beetle can make the light glow brighter if threatened by a predator.

KNOW THE GLOW!

Glowing click beetles have a taillight too! When they fly, a body part near their rear end lights up, just like an airplane.

MILLIPEDE

KNOW THE GLOW!

These millipedes are poisonous to many animals, including small **mammals**. The glow tells hungry mice and others to skip this millipede meal!

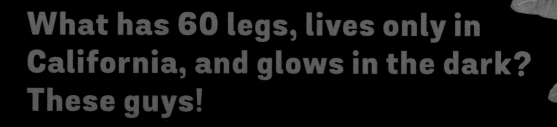

What has 60 legs, lives only in California, and glows in the dark? These guys!

- Millipedes are long and thin with large numbers of legs. Only the *Motyxia* millipedes glow.

- They are blind! The bright glow tells predators to beware!

- Millipedes only glow at night (no surprise). In some forests, the ground can look like a starry sky as millipedes head out to feed.

SHINE TIME!

A great place to see the glowing millipedes is Sequoia National Park in central California. Look for glowing animals as you walk past some of the tallest trees in the world!

SPIDER

SHINE TIME!

Scientists found spiders that lived 100 million years ago. The spiders were trapped in amber, a kind of tree sap, that hardened over time. You can still see their glowing eyes!

Spiders seem scary to some people. Some even glow, adding to their mystery.

- Remember fluorescence (page 3)? That's what is happening with spiders.

- Shine a special black light on some types of spiders and they glow with an eerie green light.

- Spiders are not insects. They are _____. Those animals have hard outside shells called _____. The exoskeletons have parts that _____ the UV light.

wolf Spider

KNOW THE GLOW!

Wolf spiders have a different kind of glow. Like cats, the backs of their eyes reflect light. This helps them see in the dark to hunt. Shine a light at wolf spider eyes, and they glow eerily back at you!

SCORPION

SHINE TIME!

Fireflies and some of the fish in this book can turn their glow on and off. Since scorpions only **reflect** UV light, they don't switch on and off.

KNOW THE GLOW!

Scientists believe that scorpions use their whole bodies as eyes! From head to tail, they take in the light and use it to help find shelter in the dark.

Scorpions pack a powerful sting. But they also shine a strong light . . . if you have the right kind of eyes!

- Nearly all scorpions glow under UV light. That's fluorescence again! Only animals that can see UV light can see the glow.

- Scorpions live in desert areas. They have long, pointed, poisonous stingers at the end of their tails to capture their prey . . . or defend themselves.

- Why do scorpions glow? Scientists just don't really know!

GLOWING GULPER EEL

SHINE TIME!

That long tail can be a hassle. It is so long that as it whips around, it can sometimes end up tied in a knot!

Here, fishy, fishy! The tail of this long, big-mouthed eel glows like a lure.

- Though called an eel, this is really a ray-finned fish. The tip of its long tail can glow pink or red. Gulpers are about 3 ft. (.9 m) long.

- They can open their huge mouths to scoop up sand and filter out crabs and little creatures.

- Gulpers live in the very deep ocean; one was seen more than 1 mi. (1.6 km) deep!

KNOW THE GLOW!

The moray is another type of eel that glows. It can make its body turn mostly fluorescent green. Scientists think this helps it attract mates.

DINOFLAGELLATE

SHINE TIME!

When fish start eating the plankton, the bright glow may attract a bigger fish that eats the plant-eating fish!

KNOW THE GLOW!

Another type of this critter lives in the water off Baja California in Mexico. Snorkelers who have floated through the display say it's like swimming through glowing fairy dust!

Too tiny to see when they're alone, these microscopic plants brighten up the dark ocean when they gather in the millions.

- Dinoflagellates are plankton. Those are types of very, very tiny plants that live in the ocean.

- This particular kind glows blue. At night, ocean waves make a patch of glowing dinoflagellates dance with light.

- They live in just a few warm water places. In one spot off Puerto Rico, you can make a glowing path through the water with your kayak.

Micro view of Dinoflagellate

FOXFIRE FUNGUS

SHINE TIME!

The same chemicals in fireflies and fish make these fungi glow!

What's that glowing green in the dark forest? Did some fairies leave the light on? No, it's just fungus!

- Fungus is not a plant or animal. Mushrooms are a type of fungus.

- More than 70 types of fungus glow green at night using bioluminescence.

- Some scientists think the fungi glow to attract insects. Like bees spreading pollen, the insects spread the of the fungi. That helps more fungi grow!

KNOW THE GLOW!

These glowing types of mushroom grow on rotting wood on the forest floor.

GLOSSARY

arachnids: a group of animals with hard outer shells that includes spiders and scorpions

bacteria: also called germs, are microscopic organisms not visible with the naked eye

bioluminescence: light created by living creatures

chemical reaction: changing matter at its atomic level

colonies: collections of very small animals that make up a larger organism

digestive system: the body parts that change food into energy

dorsal: on an animal's back

echinoderms: small, marine animals that don't have a spine or backbone

exoskeleton: an animal's hard outer shell

fluorescence: a type of light that appears to glow rather than shine

invertebrates: animals that do not have spines or backbones

larvae: a juvenile form of an insect following its birth from an egg

mammals: animals that have hair, live babies, and nurse with milk

nudibranch: a mollusk without a shell in the adult state and without true gills